Stef Mo is the performing poetry  writer Stefan Mohamed, like wh special situation-specific armou: or Parisian Subterfuge Batman, London but he's from mid-Wale this is the future, in which case h has performed poetry in a pub, in a field, in a yurt, in a living room and somewhere inside London's Roundhouse. His novels *Bitter Sixteen* and *Ace of Spiders* are published by Salt Publishing.

C000179052

Panic!

Stef Mo

Burning Eye

This edition published by Burning Eye Books 2016

www.burningeye.co.uk
@burningeyebooks

Burning Eye Books
15 West Hill, Portishead, BS20 6LG

ISBN 978 1 90913 674 8

For Cath, for helping me not to panic (too much)

Contents

I Have a Gun   9

Small Talk   12

Let's Be Friends   14

Confession   16

Love Poem #2   19

Overheard Bus Conversation Haiku   20

In Spoons   21

A Lovely Springtime Walk   24

Dystopia   26

Falafel   28

Just a Light Lunch :-)   31

Wargames, Part I   33

Pasty Envy (Wargames, Part II)   35

Absolutely Stinkin' Rancid Rich   37

Meh (Indie Nihilism)   39

Love Poem #1   41

The National Anthem   43

Clubbing   45

Panic!   47

Partly Political Broadcast on Behalf of the WTF Party   50

Possibly Racist Haiku About Mermaids   53

Space Dust of the Mind   54

Love Poem #5   57

Dance   59

Again   62

3652   65

The Boy Who Fell Off the World   67

She   69

Cameron's Britain   73

Existentially Troubling Cat Gif Haiku   77

Motivational Speaking   78

Monkey with a Flamethrower (for a Face)   81

A List of Things I Saw on the Way to a Wedding I Didn't
Want to Go To   83

Wake Up Sheeple   86

Revolution   89

Passive-Aggressive Haiku Left in Engineering Bay of
Starship   90

Wisdom Teeth   91

Human Stuff   100

The Last Sunrise   103

Before Autumn   108

In Case of Emergency, Break Haiku   110

I Have a Gun

I have a gun!
A foam rocket put-a-sock-in-it launcher
with attached mega water pistol
stop what yer doin' I said cease and desist'll gun.
A laser phaser Taser blazer master blaster (jammin') slammin'
wham bam thank you ma'am nothing to lose don't give a damn
stand up straight and protect the fam
here and now
blaww blaww blaww
ker-pow
gun.
A *we had a playground battle and I won* gun.
Not a *police department FREEZE* gun
not a *finish gang-related arguments with ease* gun
not a *lie down on the floor don't sing SCREAM* gun.
Like Martin Luther King had a dream
I have... a gun.
And I won't hesitate to use it.
But, unlike many who claim to subscribe to Dr King's dream
I shall not abuse it.
Well... maybe a bit.
But it's fine if the person doin' the abusin' is someone you trust, innit?
You're safe snoozin' while your favourite abuser's
all, like, abusin' for the greater good 'n' shit?
Pfft! I am not here for moral implications and ramifications.
I have a gun.
Not an armed bank robbery
gimme 'nuff respec' yobbery
and other such knobbery gun.
Not a badass accessory to go with my slobbery dog gun *doggone it*

this my lawn and you ain't supposed to be upon it gun.

As a stun gun would stun a glum nun 'til she woke up even more
numb and bummed, this fun gun would send her on a fun run
with her estranged mum and her estranged mum's strange son
politely reunited and squirting tequila, deal her a new habit
run rabbit run rabbit run run run here I come with my gun gun gun
I'm gonna
what
this gun is
not
gonna shoot bullets
when I pull it (how boring).
I'll keep this gun under my pillow so I can record my snoring.
This gun becomes a brolly when the rain is pouring.
This gun will make you jolly if you start yawning.
This gun shoots a small flag with 'BANG' written on it, that's ace
but
if a coyote turned it on himself it *would* shoot him in the face
but
he would survive –
this gun works on cartoon logic
a cel-shaded operating system
and if you tried to actually shoot anyone with it
it would deliberately miss them.
This gun is **SO BIG** I need an entourage to carry it.
This gun is *so small* a Noisy Cricket would want to marry it.
I have a gun
and I'm a bit afraid to use it
'cause it knows not what it do.
This gun is not a metaphor
for a better war
meta to the core, it's

10

glittering, instinctive, it's
not as clever as it thinks it is
not what you might think it is
not what I might say it is
not cool (by the way – it is)
it's *not* a gun
it's a *lotta* gun
and you have never clapped eyes on a *hotter* gun.
I have a gun and it's under control.
I have a gun and it's rock and it's roll.
I have a gun built by the keenest clown.
I have a gun that'll bring you back to life when you need it
like a Phoenix Down.
I have a gun that shoots smooth grooves and soothes.
I have a gun of which the NRA does not approve.
I have a gun for which, when you *absolutely positively gotta amuse*
    every motherfucker in the room, you should accept no substitutes.
I have a gun that has only positive attributes.
I have a gun that will not win battles through murder
or forcing surrender or retreats.
I have a gun that will render any battle you've ever heard of obsolete.
I have a gun that's sometimes shaped like a mic.
I have a gun you can borrow.
If you like.

Small Talk

I wish things weren't so awkward.
We've faced apocalypses together, stood
shoulder to bleeding shoulder
backs to bloodied wall
facing down howling hordes, armed
with nothing
but bruised fists
shit-eating grins
and camaraderie
yet sit us together in the same living room
with an afternoon to kill
and it's like a first date between two people
who are only doing it
because they share some really pushy mutual friends.
I spend too much time fiddling
with tea and coffee-making paraphernalia
and you keep sort-of-but-not-really reading
an old *Guardian* Culture section
and small talk chokes and chugs
like an old machine
and I watch dying cells dive off my arm
like the last hurrah of some suicide cult
and I still can't remember if you take sugar.
So we end up just... sitting.
And if anyone asked, I know we'd both swear the silence
is companionable
although we both know it really, really isn't
and I don't think I've ever been more relieved
to see a grenade hurtling through an open window.

God

I think I was actually just about to ask you
something about football.

Let's Be Friends

Let's be friends.

Let's paint each other's faces like Power Rangers, then try to get a loan for something serious.

Let's skive off work and leave ransom notes on our desks saying we've been kidnapped by our inner children.

Let's go at the clocks with hammers and tweezers and plutonium rods and create mini time paradoxes, and sell them out of the back of your van.

Let's be friends.

Let's stumble in from a club at four in the morning and crack open a fresh bottle of rum, secure in the knowledge that it's not just a good idea but *the best idea*.

Let's climb that tree and see which one of us can reach that cloud above it that's shaped like a fish. It is shaped like a fish. It *is* shaped like a fish. Look! There's the tail, there's the... it *is* shaped like a fish! How about *you* shut up? You... fine. Fine. Fine! Let's just climb the stupid tree.

Let's be friends.

Let's enable one another's self-indulgence and sip from one another's cups of particular, peculiar psychosis.

Let's hide on the roof of the community centre during a UKIP meeting and throw things at people as they leave, and then next week one of us can do a totally unironic Facebook status about how even if we totally disagree with someone else's political viewpoint, we have to be tolerant and respectful because tolerance and freedom of speech and stuff, etc., and the other one can Like it, also unironically.

Let's be friends.

Let's have already been friends for a really long time, and also have been alive for longer than we've been alive, and then in the future we can tell our kids about how we saw Nirvana and Blur and Radiohead in the nineties at those epoch-defining gigs, and our kids can be like *oh shut up, you old shits, no one cares about your naff old instrument bands, I'm trying to download the latest pirate glittercore mashups into my neuroflaps.* And I can be like *ugh I hate my kids* and you can be like *me too, I hate your kids too. And my kids.* And I can be like *haha yeah. I hate your kids too.*

Let's be friends.

Let's sit and have a conversation where our voices get steadily louder and our gestures more and more expansive, until we're asked to leave the restaurant, and then let's apologise and leave politely, 'cause we're not dicks, but also 'cause it's a crap restaurant. Sorry, bad choice on my part. Thanks for being so nice about it, though.

Let's sit and watch the sun come up and have a conversation that mostly consists of the phrases *what were we talking about* and *I don't know,* and copious giggling.

Let's sit on the doorstep in supportive silence when something bad happens, and share a cigarette, even though neither of us smokes any more.

Let's be friends.

Let's agree that if we ever got involved in a fight for whatever reason we would both utterly wipe the floor with whoever picked it, even though we both know we can't fight for shit in real life, and we also hate fighting.

Let's have had each other's backs at school and unapologetically wish *actual literal brutal death* upon anyone who gave us a hard time, reminding one another that it's fine, because there's no such thing as karma and no one's listening AND IT'S FINE, OK?

Let's be sure to remember that if one of us dies unexpectedly and/or poetically.

Let's be friends.

Confession

We're not entirely sure what you are, exactly
but we know we don't like you.
It's frustrating
not being able to pin it down properly.
From the first notes of the register
it's clear that something is amiss:
Davies. Davies. Davies. Davies.
Evans. Evans.
Jones. Jones. Jones. Jones. Jones. Jones.
... Mohamed.
Trigger warning: *He's not from round 'ere.*
But the name thing isn't... I mean...
it's a useful shorthand, definitely. You've got to understand
that we're really having to feel our way here.
That's why it took so long to realise
that chanting *MOHAMED ALI*
wasn't really an insult.
We think there might be something a bit Jewish going on too
judging by your nose
and something we heard from someone somewhere
which is also confusing. I mean...
what even *is* a Jewish?

But we do want to make it clear that the kid who called you a Paki
was acting alone.
Even we're not that stupid.

To be honest
it's not even a race thing, really.
One of our best friends is literally black.
And he doesn't like you either.

It's just easier to focus on racial aspects
because while we do know, intellectually
that fundamentally
we just distrust everything about you
and hate you on a really basic level
that's kind of hard to articulate
and process into nice, sharp, compact soundbites
to throw at you in the changing rooms
or in the corridors
which is why it's really handy when you let your hair grow long.
It gives us something to grab hold of. No pun intended! Haha.
And we do know that you don't fancy boys
but again, GAY! is just really *easy*, y'know?
Ultimately, I think the problem is
that as a collective livestock hivemind thing
we just can't deal with how utterly awesome you are.
The armoured unicorn you ride to school.
The way girls flock to you, irresistibly drawn
by your pulsating, glowing personal magnetism.
Your snappy comebacks
which would have made you a local legend
even if you *weren't* the only person
within a one-hundred-and-fifty-mile radius
with an Islamic surname.
The way you swaggered on stage at the school dance
and absolutely *shredded* that Hendrix solo
on that cool-as-shit electric guitar that you built yourself
in Technology.

It's all just a bit too much for us to process.

So this is just to let you know
that when we all stampede after you

we only want to beat you up
to demonstrate our deep, overpowering love
for everything that you represent.
It's the only way
that we can express it.
Also by throwing eggs.
And if you should happen to escape
by doing a totally awesome somersault over the fence
and then running along the other side of the fence
righteously showering us with middle-fingered salutes
in a totally awesome way
like, in such a way that you'll still be dining out on the story
more than ten years later
we won't be angry.
We'll just *look* really angry
because our facial muscles are not yet developed enough
to communicate that level of awestruckness.
Seriously. You rock.

Or you're a long-haired Jewish Muslim poof.
To be honest, we don't even know any more.

Love Poem #2

Oh my God

you're like a brand new air freshener spraying the scent of peach
cocktails on a lavender beach on the shores of a velvet sea into the
filth-encrusted boarding school toilet of my life

you're both the Ls in a gigantic LOL written on the sky in rainbow-
coloured smoke by a pink loop-the-looping biplane that will shortly
spontaneously explode from the sheer intensity of the LOL and the
pilot's parachute will open and it's a gigantic flaming heart that
guides him down into a champagne hot tub full of naked
supermodels

you're the impact of the punch that Will Smith delivers to the face of
that alien in *Independence Day*, and also the awesomeness of the way
he says *Welcome to Earth* and then pops a cigar in his mouth

OMFG
I want to eat you and never digest you so you're inside me 4 alwayz

I WANT TO LEARN MARTIAL ARTS AND MAKE A LIST OF
EVERYBODY WHO HAS EVER WRONGED YOU AND TRACK
DOWN AND BRUTALLY AND CREATIVELY SLAUGHTER ALL
BUT ONE OF THEM AND I WILL THEN PIN THE MURDERS ON
THE ONE WHO IS LEFT OVER

Jesus H Billygoat-Riding Christ Emmanuel Our Father Who Art in
Heaven is a Halfpipe halfway there living in Aberdare
if this truly is love then I think maybe you need to cut me off
'cause I'm totally going to have a heart attack if this carries on.

Overheard Bus Conversation Haiku

Let's talk later, some
guy's writing down everything
we say. Proper weird.

In Spoons

I'm sat in Wetherspoons
at 10 am
surrounded by 10 am Wetherspoons guys.
Those old guys.
You know the type.
And I'm all dilated-eyed
from being up all night
although *not* from drugs, funnily enough
not from drugs.
Didn't fancy having all the rugs pulled out from under me
and chundering under the weight of my own
profundity.
So I exaggerate a stumble up to the bar
and order a non-alcoholic beer
which I'll drink from a brown paper bag
in the hope that it looks appropriately queer.
And I'll discuss Iraq with a yellow-palmed Jack in a paedophile mac
and refuse his offer of crack, 'cause I have standards.
Even in Wetherspoons.
Even at 10 am.

It's me and them.

And all I want to do is resume my activity
i.e. mining a particularly English seam of eccentricity
one that simply wouldn't be practical for any other ethnicity
i.e. going to work at the BBC after three tabs of LSD
and commissioning a new puppet show
about a tramp who lives in a tree

then buggering off at half past three for fish, chips, mushy peas
and a cup of tea
except
this isn't 1973
and I'll probably end up interviewing
potential reality show participants
for ITV.
A fate truly worse than death.

I take a deep breath.
This is nonsense.
And not a good place for discussing career options.

Verse two, and I wonder what voodoo
turned that geezer's feelers
blue.
Give me a clue. Please. Do.
And who put Luke Goss
on the jukebox?
I might
puke.
Lots.
And I'm nuke-hot
from my head to the toes of my
puce socks.
And why am I wearing
puce socks?
And come to think of it
does Spoons even *have*
a jukebox?
And why do they keep the
juice locked

up?
Man. I haven't had a drop.
Fucked.

This place is nuts.
That guy's drinking with his eyes shut.
That guy's coughing his guts up.
That guy doesn't even talk. He clucks.
Another Newcastle Brown, Chuck?
Bwck bwck bwck.
And that guy's head's all weird and soft
and I'm sitting here
hoping some of this weirdness
is going to rub off
on me.

But verse three
is worse, me
sat here
with this flat beer
surrounded by lonely-eyed alcoholics
whose lives resemble
endlessly repeating bad dreams.
And it seems like I should say
who are you to judge me?
to myself
on their behalf.
And I think I need to go home
and have a warm bath.
And stop inspiring
weird looks
from the bar staff.

A Lovely Springtime Walk

Ah, the smell of freshly cut grass
refreshing, intoxicating, invigorating
can mean only one thing

the human pestilence still lingers on

I mean... ah...
Springtime brings springtime flings!
Golden sunshine in concentric rings!
Happy little birds that sing
and flap their lovely wings!
We are all queens and kings!
Hello house! Hello mouse!

*Hello cheating louse, soused
on Famous Grouse at his mistress's house
watching House on Netflix*

hello lovely trees and sticks!
AAAH I feel very sick
ignore the pain
and focus
on the click
my heels
so light and carefree on the tarmac. Cat!

I'll eat it like the sarlacc

Garlic
on the wind (mmm)
hello church! Bless me, Father (though I have not sinned)
and bless *you*, Father (and your many chins)

I feel as though a potion of alcoholic lotion, acid, razor blades
and past-its-sell-by-date fermented COW
IS BUBBLING
IN MY STOMACH NOW
sweat is curdling on my brow

24

HELLO FARMER!

Did you repair your plough?

Ow! I mean... oh!

That's really very good to know

now back through your fields you can safely roam. Excuse me!

For I must get home.

> *Gyrating salivating like a horse that's gnawing at the bit*
> *doubled over like I need a shSTAND UP STRAIGHT*
> *NOBODY CAN GUESS THE NATURE*
> *OF YOUR STATE*

HELLO PEOPLE AT THE BUS STOP

I hope you don't have long to wait!

Ah, typical, here come three at once

*see you soon you bunch of cu*NSTABLE! Good afternoon!

A boy! You must be over the moon!

No, I'm fine! Stomach bug! Really does pull the rug

from under one! No, not much fun! Goodbye! Ah!

HELLO PARK, HELLO LARK!

HELLO PROTONS, HELLO QUARKS!

Ah

relief

home at last

better sort this fast

> *recalibrate you berk*
> *wrong flesh setting*
> *no wonder it didn't work*

ah, that's better

far more stable

far more comfy

far more able.

Back in my synthetic suit of man.

> *The invasion will proceed as planned.*

Dystopia

Slipping through the dystopian murk
>> tripping on some plutonium quirk
>>>> I listen to the harmonium smirk
>> light-headed as the petroleum spurts.
With every toke I become more of a berk
>> (*smokin' don't always make you alert*)
>>>> you think I'm a joke as I lurk
>> like you've never seen a bloke in a skirt.

If only you'd heard me herd those herds of absurd verbs
>> a shepherd whose disturbing, unheard-of words
>> pack more pith than an orange, more shit than a sturdy turd
and enough puckered-lip fuckery to make a lemon murder its own
>>>> curd.
I'm like Tyler Durden, if he was a nerd.

(*Except not quite as tough, not quite as buff, not quite as psychologically fucked and not quite as made up. And stuff.*)

My circle of friends ain't much. We've got a creature
>> made of belly button fluff
>>>> who calls himself the Jellied Mutton Brush
>> a banker who's recently been sleeping rough
and a wanker who we can't get rid of.
>> Or 'of whom we can't get rid'.
>>>> Just 'cause one time I lent him a quid.
>> And last but not least we have
an ego and an id
>> an eagle and a squid
>>>> and an evil little kid

26

and if I told you what he did

to the weevil we called Sid

you'd think it was a trick

but still probably be sick.

Anyway

this munting collective spits munting invective

infected by their various disgusting perspectives

eating stale digestives in a manner suggestive

of beings who simply aren't interested

in being divested

of the deranged, debased and distasteful

perplexingly wasteful and

profoundly hateful wastrel ways they practise in their

post-apocalyptic caves...

(*Sorry. That sentence nearly got away.*)

So if you've been following this tale and swallowing this tale
you can't help but pinpoint the moral in this tale.

Though I shan't say it. To relay it

would both rob it of its elegance and most *grievously* insult your

intelligence.

Falafel

I'm having an out-of-body experience
that is inextricably
and inexplicably
interknotted
with the word
falafel.
I am lying, warmly frozen, at the epicentre
of a time-delayed sub-bass throb, all foetal
like a Star Child born in the eternity
between the breakdown and the drop
and I'm enjoying the way my teeth and tongue
are causing the word
falafel
to mutate.
Faaaaalafel.
faLAfel.
flfl.
LEFALAF.

And I'm also floating, lightweight, fat and untethered
beyond the peaks of the trees, watching myself down there
enjoying the word
falafel
but also enjoying my down-there self's enjoyment of the word
falafel
but from a more detached, analytical perspective.
Like, down there it's a combination
of appreciating the sound of the word
falafel
and also just a full four-jawed chomping kind of

faaaaaaLAFAAAL
like saying the word
falafel
is becoming what it's like to eat a
falafel
like an om-nom-nomatopoeia.
Very tactile. Primal.
Faaaaaaaaaaaalafel.
But then there's the first level of out-of-bodiness
up there (or here)
deconstructing the image of me enjoying
the munching and mangling and mastication
(and likely also enjoying the alliteration)
and also enjoying the random confluence of events
and thoughts and gestures and chemical reactions
that has led to me being down there
mutilating the word
falafel
while also enjoying that mutilation from further away
but anyway that's a bit of a closed loop.

... But wait.
It goes deeper.

'Cause while there's me down here (or down there)
and me up here (or up there)
I'm also now aware of being *here*
writing about the two-pronged multi-consciousness that I've become
munching the word
falafel
and also intellectually appreciating the many levels
on which both the word

29

falafel

and the enjoyment of the word

falafel

and even the very nature, history and meaning of the word

falafel

operate

and I'm sitting here writing, and as I write I become aware

that I'm standing *here*, reading what I'm writing (or what I've
    written)

sitting there, about being up here (or there), observing myself

down there (or down here), these four (or maybe more) levels

of me exploring the semantic, metaphysical and pronunciational

aspects of the word

falafel

and I'm *so* close to the EUREKA moment

the revelation

the catharsis of ultimate enlightenment

I can see it

it's there

it's there

it's... it's... it's... it's...

... gone.

And all I can remember

is the word

falafel.

And I can't get it out

of my head.

And I don't know why.

And it's annoying.

Just a Light Lunch :-)

Feast (no pun intended) your eyes
on this aggressively sumptuous
yet subtly flirtatious
honeymoon weekend
of Mediterranean herb-garnished
duck and venison double helix
stuffed to bursting point
with an invading army
of fricasséed pork nuggets
autumnal vegetable clusters
and spice-sweetened cheese revelations
garlanded by gooseflesh-armoured
antediluvian potato spirals
floating decadently yet modestly
on a bubbling fairytale lake
of painstakingly reverse-engineered gravy
freshened with an acid retort
of Mouton Rothschild 1945
wistfully tethered
to a tender-as-a-broken-heart
cocoon of raspberry-injected
pastry innocence
and meditatively matured
caviar flibbertigibbets
positioned with strategic precision
against a buffer zone
of molten, beef-trimmed garlic chevrons
sprinkled with a delighted child's
first snowfall of dreamlike
pule molecules.

Look at it.
Just look at it.
Look at it.
LOOK AT IT.

And don't you *dare*
to even *begin*
to *conceive*
of an *alternate reality*
in which you would *consider*
eating it.

It's not for you.

Wargames, Part I

We are making preparations
for the oncoming war.
We don't know what form it'll take
so we're thinking outside the box.
I'm stitching protective sigils
into the lining of my red fox battle onesie
you're hammering sheet metal
into grizzly bear armour
and the troops, or whatever they are
festoon their own costumes –
chipmunks, wolves, raccoons
and a skunk, for some reason –
with papier-mâché teeth and charity shop pelts
so it looks like we've already done
a bunch of killing.
We have also established a strong
online presence.
Propagandistic memes cut through newsfeeds
like hot knives through old metaphors
and Likes take on the significance of captured bases
retweeted through occupied territories
selfies processed with victorious filters
and carried on the Internet's hyperbolic siren winds
average ratings levelled to smoking rubble
by a constant barrage of brutal reviews –
but this war will not be won
on TripAdvisor alone.
Hearts and minds, people. Hearts and minds
and shock and awe
and fire and brimstone

and sugar and spice and all things nice
made nasty in tarnished bronze cauldrons.
Lacing bombs with perfume
folding jewel steel for samurai umbrellas
and corrupting grandfather clockwork
to make rapid-ageing artillery;
watch our enemies shrivel
from fresh-faced privates
to wizened, haunted veterans
in the time it takes for me to say
Got any more rosy apples?
I've run out.
Now morning's cold moon dims
and I survey the barricades
astride my fearsome Lego horse
sipping a hot milkshake
as the latest reports come in.
Our Ordnance Survey maps may be well out of date
but according to Google
it will take the enemy five hours and forty-three minutes
to get here
depending on the traffic
and whether they choose to travel by road
foot
or bicycle.
Google gives no option
for horses.

Fellows! I call. *At ease.*
Time for a spot of Crash Bandicoot
before the carnage begins.

Pasty Envy (Wargames, Part II)

It's not your pasty face that I envy
but that oh-so-tasty steak and ale pasty
with its gracefully flaking pastry
staking its claim
to the contested space
at the centre of our disgraced table
all grave and gloopy gravy
chorizo-louche and olive-lazy
flavourful, coquettish and graceful
simultaneously dead as the table
and the last truly living thing in this wasteland
this café that's actually just four barely-standing walls
and a rubble-strewn floor
door face-down like a dead clown
beneath a crumpled tragedy
of collapsed tent.
Somewhere, horsemen canter; apocalyptic clip-clop.
You're looking heavy metal. I'm feeling pretty hip-hop.
We sit
locked
in a mutually assured staring contest.
Waiting.

I have a knife. You have a bow and arrow. I have a gun. You have a
rifle and gun-proof shield. I have rifle-proof armour and a high-yield
RPG. You have a dragon gauntlet that has laid waste to so many BBC
journalists. I have an Infernalist, a four-thousand-bitcoin war crime
in waiting. You have the Diplomatic Incident, an abstract weapon of
the Discourse War. I have a psychic scroll that exposes all your flaws.
You add +5 to your Pomposity, narrowly defending against my

Highest Velocity Mega-Atrocity, as you prepare to launch your
Ununited Nations Anti-Resolution. I defend with Russell Brand's
Tactical Revolution, which doesn't actually do anything but distracts
you with vapid clickbait fluff long enough for me to eject an ace
from my sleeve
i.e. my hand
which I'll just use to swipe the pasty
and push you over
giving me ample time to run
for what remains of the hills.

... except
that I can't quite bring myself
to use so underhand a method.
The last vestige of chivalry, perhaps? The end of honour?

Whatever.

We fall back into staring, pouring silent loathing
from my face to your face and back again
my raging hook nose screaming curses
at your disingenuous button
and it seems that we'll be locked in stalemate
until the pasty just moulders away into inedibleness.

Which is frustrating.
But let's be honest –
it's not really about the pasty any more, is it?

Absolutely Stinkin' Rancid Rich

Yo Mr Tramp, Mr Shop Doorway, 'sup?
I pay a dude to pay a dude to spit into yo' beggin' cup.
And in return I'll take that smelly dog away from you!
He'll forget you in the time it takes to gobble down some proper food
(and get his dirty coat shampooed).

I'm absolutely stinkin' filthy rancid fetid *putrid* rich!
I own your gravity, I bought the patent off of Newton, bitch!
Ain't no one EVER been this stinkin' rancid fetid putrid rich!
Like Ozymandias and Rockefeller in a petri dish.

The banquets I attend are quite offensive in their majesty
unicorn falafel served with pushmi-pullyu travesty
then tenderloin of Hippogriff – the gravy? Rumpelstiltskin blood.
And haggis stuffed with firstborn, better get the fackin' kilts in, bud
(and pass the roasted angel spuds).

I'm totally, despicably, 'I spit at thee, you peasants' rich!
A million-person orchestra to advertise my presence rich!
Chalet on the moon, the bloody *spoons* are unobtainium!
The eggs are Fabergé, OK? The bloody sky is raining 'em!

Now you might say it's tacky that I do so love to rub it in.
And maybe in your grotty little council flat you're reigning king.
Keep telling everyone that I'm not *really* happy with my bling.
I'll ponder it while glamour girls snort fairy dust from off my thing.
Now shut your hole and hear me sing:

I'm absolutely stinkin' filthy rancid fetid *putrid* rich!
Bloated, gloating, who-needs-voting, bow down to the new kid rich!

Selling futures – literally! I bought myself a time machine!
A Pimp-My-Fackin'-TARDIS, mate, those fackin' Time Lords
work for me!

I'm utterly, disgustingly, gut-bustingly, I'm – trust me – rich!
The wolf of all streets, horny lord whose feet are never crusty, rich!
Maybe money can't buy love, but who needs love when you can buy
a spaceship? Keep your shitty world! I'm off to claim another! Bye!

Meh (Indie Nihilism)

I'm a rebel.

Rancid ramshackle reprobate raving with a risible raygun.

Chewing on shock Tic Tacs.

Rocking a misspelled *Fukc Evrythnig* T-shirt.

Picking at my temporary transfer tattoo, head in a chicken bucket.

Sticking pins in some voodoo pervert puppet.

This is my post-postmodern punk project™, my

penetrative, pejorative performance, you can't

process the power of my pranged-out poetry, as I

proudly pump pungent and petrifyingly profound

pragmatism pancakes into your processing unit with the

preternatural panache of a precognitive primate. I'm a

psychopathic pilot. The People's Pirate. Kicking

fifty shades

of seven bells

out of acid-bellied pilled-up farewells

in piss-tearful stairwells

a kryptonite crack binge

with a swamp shark syringe.

I'm ones and zeroes.

Cyber drifter. Escaped shapeshifter.

I am a broken hyperlink.

A tub of virtual oven cleaner for your avatar to drink.

I'm *meh*.

I'm the Melancholic Endgame of Hedonism.

I'm Monumental. Ermahgerd. Hell on a stick.

I'm Me = Everything. Huh.

I'm buh *buh* buh *buh buh* buh *buh*.

I'm savage like the spurts of a syphilitic skunk

sozzled on salacious scorpion stings

and other unsanitary things.

No saving *me* with a saline solution.

I Alien spit on your praline pollution.

A pox on your chocolate box dinner party revolution.

I'm appropriating inappropriate Shakespeare references

adding

then deleting them

from first drafts.

I'm *anti*-second drafts.

And pro-anti-craft.

There's no name for my movement.

Why would the emperor tell you where his groove went?

Turn up the distortion

clowns cowering in craven contortions

as we shrug

abort any thoughts of caution

and blow miniscule things clean out of proportion's orbit.

Laugh in the face

of the government's UN-approved Hadouken blast.

Calmly absorb it.

Didn't get a train to the march

'cause I COULDN'T BLOODY AFFORD IT.

I'm a rebel. I'm roaring.

I'm an out-of-context quotation

on a Condescending Wonka drawing.

I'm out of my shell. Ninja snail.

#pisspoorpunkproject.

Epic fail.

Love Poem #1

Boy meets girl.

Boy likes girl (but is afraid to say so).

Girl likes boy (but is afraid to say so).

Boy's friends say he should go for it.

Girl's friends say she should go for it.

Boy and girl spend time together, but any attempts to develop their
relationship from platonic to romantic are consistently thwarted
by supernatural occurrences.

Boy and girl attempt, with varying degrees of success, to balance
their mutual attraction with their need to battle their own
personal demons, as well as actual demons, monsters, robots,
shadowy government conspiracies etc.

Girl gets turned evil.

Boy fights girl.

Girl goes back to normal.

Boy and girl pursue tentative romance but things are weird.

Boy's evil ex comes to town and starts brutally murdering people in
ways that chillingly echo episodes in their relationship.

Girl's all like *wut*.

Boy's like *meargh*.

Boy and girl eventually defeat boy's evil ex but their relationship
stalls.

Girl's evil clone seduces boy, putting further strain on their
relationship.

Boy and girl agree to spend time apart, but are miserable and their
friends are all like *for God's sake sort it out, you dicks*.

Girl goes to tell boy how she really feels but on the way she is
transported to a parallel universe.

Boy thinks girl is dead, starts drinking and takes up with girl's friend.

Girl reappears weeks later but she has aged seventy years due to time running differently in the parallel universe.

Boy must decide whether he can still love girl now that she's all old and wrinkly and shit.

Girl reappears, and it turns out that the old version of her is actually an evil monster, and the real girl is still young and HOT.

Boy and girl defeat evil monster and are about to get it on when girl finds out about boy and her friend.

Boy tries to explain that he thought she was all, like, dead and shit and he was grieving and not thinking straight but she's totally distraught and is having none of it.

Boy and girl's on-off relationship takes a back seat for a while and loads of other crazy shit goes down in the meantime including a plague that makes all the children super strong AND INSANE, and an army of robot alien vampire Republicans.

Boy and girl start to get closer and it seems like they're finally going to get together when a huge apocalyptic event goes down, and there's all, like, fighting and drama and shit, and it all looks hopeless, and there's a massive cliffhanger.

Network execs cancel series before cliffhanger can be resolved.

Series creator takes to Kickstarter and raises enough money for a one-off TV movie in which all loose ends are wrapped up.

Boy and girl finally get together, except it's a different actress playing the girl because of scheduling conflicts, and it's all a bit anticlimactic, and critics pan it, and the fans hate it and are extremely vocal about how much they hate it on the Internet.

It's the age-old story.

The National Anthem

God save British values

God save doublethink

God save an unfair hearing

God save secret courts

God save smear campaigns

God save wilful misinterpretation

God save gleeful distortion of the facts

God save me from having to think for myself

God save the echo chamber

God save the narrative

God save the ability to eat a bacon sandwich convincingly

God save the race to the bottom

God save front-page cellulite reveals and bikini body countdowns

God save guilty even if proven innocent

God save mindless jingoism

God save the centre ground

God save vacuous press releases

God save triangulated policy statements

God save shiny media watering holes

God save blood-soaked cocaine, expensive champagne and cold
passionless sex with someone called Sebastian

God save financial speculation

God save derivatives

God save our AAA credit rating! ... oops

God save an ex-empire state of mind

God save benefit sanctions

God save crumbling tower blocks

God save my unlimited-edition austerity boxer shorts

God save a pint of piss

God save the empathy deficit

God save the Overton window

God save lefty infighting

God save twatsplaining

God save SINGING ALONG WHETHER YOU WANT TO OR NOT

God save whoever killed satire

God save looking out for number one

God save pulling the ladder up behind you

God save unchecked privilege

God save unrestrained prejudice

God save untapped potential

God save that racist taxi driver, 'cause to be fair to him he did know
    the quickest route back to my house from the bus station

God save hypocrisy so blatant that it's like a crowbar to the ribs

God save Pudsey the fucking dog.

Clubbing

We're in da club.
Soaking on this spinning spit, tripping through the dripping pit of
sausagecock-swinging spunk slingers, a triple-dick recession
procession singing premature victory songs, the bantersome captains
of the Muntington Mongers, Gash Gordon and Fuck Rogers,
impoverished pseudopod cephaloposh imposters, preposterous with
testosterone, shoulda stayed in Gloucester, probably, *woulda been
your loss, boss, follow me*!
We're in da club.
Desperately hammering our Spam-coloured fists at the gated ham
flaps of the cavern of tits, zomboid dudes looming and drooling cruel
and unusual ooze on an Argos catalogue's worth of bubbling boobs,
each a perfumed moon to claim and groom with our loony tools,
lunar pubes for rocket fuel, whack it in a sock for the pocket duel, a
fetid flash in a putrid pan like the cash in the crack of our rancid
pants, having a hashtagged slash with a beef bash chaser,
splashdance, race yer, best keep pace or I'll smash yer face, yeah,
wheyyyyyyyyyyyyyyy mashuppadaplace.
We're in da club.
Flexing our dreck-flecked pecs, drenched in sweat, six parts Jäger
to four parts sex, we're Ian Fury and the Cockheads, molly-swaddled
mingbrain mess cadets on a Knobber Phett rush, busted up on lumps
of untrustworthy garden shed ghost-unbuster dust, trust us bruv,
these bumps of crusty rust are Doves but not as we know 'em, let's
see who can breed with the most receded penis, that'll show 'em,
make 'em glow, if they don't blow they'd best get to know, yo.
We're in da club.
This is not a test, this is collapsing flesh spilling from V-necks and
barely-there dresses, entirely unfettered and wetter than freshly sea-
soaked Irish setters, come live in my sandwich, it's moistened bread

and meat with no lettuce, give me four letters, consonant, vowel and two more consonants, take me back to the human consulate, I need repatriating before I am absorbed into this tapestry of busted guts blood and assorted mingled mismatched nuts and other people's private stuff, shoulders where knees should be, buttocks muttering next to stomachs that stutter with glee, joyful tears secreted from the vagina between our ears, chundering bums and thumbs plunging hungrily into spongey clunges, a pulsating gyrating popping lava bed of disintegrating bodies, blubbersome and stinking like freshly shat sin with all the plastic cups, discarded bras, overturned bins and floor-hugging filth mixed in, we gurgle from DJ booth to toilet and become one once again with our own spit and piss, this is our territory now and no non-gestalt shall be allowed in, we are collective slop, orgasmic organism glistening, what a cretinous gelatinous fabulous mess we're in, an endless feedback loop of sunken eyes and nipples and jism, we have evolved through a throwback prism, soundtracked by post-pop squawk house and made green with toxic spirits, *is iiiit*, yeah, it is.
We are da club.

Now wash your hands.

Panic!

Liberals want full access to rich successful people's bank accounts so that they can transfer wildly disproportionate proportions of their money to feckless boozing layabouts to spend on Sky TV and Special Brew and cheap condoms that will break thereby leading to the impregnation of more feckless boozing layabouts whose feckless boozing babies will be nothing but a burden on the state.

Conservatives want every tenth pound earned by poor people to go to randomly-determined rich people as a thank-you for the trickle-down effect and to make sure the rich people don't take their business elsewhere and any poor people who refuse to pay or who are too poor to pay will be forced to work as slaves for said rich people in exchange for Special Brew.

Liberals think that in order to get benefits – which should be at least £4,000 per week – all you should have to do is send a text to a free number every six months promising that you are looking for work and the text doesn't even have to be in *English*.

Conservatives think that every time a new person signs on for said benefits, the amount they – and everyone else – receive should go down by at least 20 per cent until benefits just disappear entirely leaving everyone to either *get a job* or *leave the country* or just *die*.

Liberals want to force children and household pets into homosexual interspecies halal marriages.

Conservatives want everybody in the country to be partnered off into government-sanctioned heterosexual pairs who will then be married without possibility of parole and expected to have dispassionate functional intercourse at a predetermined time every other fortnight to ensure propagation of the species although conservatives also think the government should stay out of people's private business.

Liberals want to move you – yes, *you* – out of your house and into a scummy B&B so that an *immigrant* family can move into your house and their nineteen children can replace all the plumbers and handymen and corner shop proprietors in the locality and if you don't like it then you're *racist* and a *Nazi* and *must be stopped* free speech be *damned*.

Conservatives want anybody whose skin is darker than 'mocha' to supply *documentary evidence* that a) they have lived in the UK for at least twice as long as their nearest fair-skinned neighbour and that b) they make a noticeable contribution to the country's GDP or face deportation to a randomly selected continent where darker-skinned people are the majority.

Liberals want a profligate and sprawling NHS whose hospitals will double as *taxpayer-funded* old people's homes funded *by the taxpayer*.

Conservatives just want everybody to grow a backbone and stiffen up their upper lip and stop whinging and then there'd be no *need* for an NHS!

Liberals want to force you – yes, *you*, and all the decent hard-working law-abiding tax-paying women you know (as well as all the decent hard-working law-abiding tax-paying women you *don't* know) – to have abortions and the aborted foetuses will be fed intravenously to old people to make them live longer and *continue* to be a burden on the state but the old people will also be euthanised as soon as they stop being useful (under the guise of 'compassion') oh and liberals also say the old people will go nowhere when they die because there is no heaven they'll just rot and their remains will be dug up and eaten by the foxes that are overrunning the country since the bloody fox hunting ban came in and they want this *taught in our schools our decent hard-working taxpayer-funded schools*!

Conservatives want *chastity belts* for all women and *womb cameras* controlled by their fathers or other male guardians and for old people to just *die* and stop being a burden on the state but to also be forced to stay alive when their quality of life is basically *torture* and they want a new king of Britain to head up the British Reich and finally *nuke those frog-guzzling European communist socialist bastards* before said communist socialist bastards force everybody to speak German and Islamic and eat frogs and pay for Polish cleaners to stay at home and not clean anything and watch Sky TV paid for *BY THE TAXPAYER* the *decent hard-working law-abiding striving pasty-eating quiet-pint-of-beer-drinking bingo-playing family-estate-car-driving taxpayer*!

Sigh.

Partly Political Broadcast on Behalf of the WTF Party

I stand before you enhumbled and gigantified
pre-, de-, un- and re-toxified
Twitter-proof and lion-hearted
here to finish what they started
yes, they've started so I'll finish
freshly varnished, undiminished
quaffing the salt of the earth from my silver spoon
and swearing true before each of you
that I will paint a Union Jack on the moon.

Bend over before this prodigy, sum of nineteen centuries
of Anglo-Saxon progeny, allow me
to roger thee with jollity, footloose and policy-free, I promise thee
Bakewell tarts and French (but not *French*) fancies for all!
We shall split London in half with a new *Mer*lin Wall!
Proper British brickwork formed in the heat of St George's forge
dragon breath adhesive from the fairytale gorge.
Sit and have a pint with this front-bench-pressing Ford Corsair
engaged in political trench warfare
challenging the cosmopolitan liberal-conservative orthodoxy
(you can vote by post or by proxy)
join me for English fish, British pommes-frites
mushy gawd-blimey-crikey-Blighty peas
and hot sweet builder's tea from our Home Counties plantation
as I address ye, my ye olde congregation.
With you as my witnesses, and with no exaggeration
I shall further divide this divided nation!

Hate thy neighbour! No ifs, no buts!
It's a national pastime, let's go nuts!

Why mince words? Say, *Hey, get stuffed!*
Hey guy, gay guy, straight guy, *rrruff!*
Blue guy, Jew guy, white guy, bright guy
sick guy, thick guy, proud guy, loud guy
brown guy, black guy, red guy, head guy
screw these live guys, screw those dead guys!
Whether they're their guys or our guys, near guys or far guys
(oh, and also women, but we don't really talk about them –
orders from our PR guys!).

Golly gosh, fie, pish, fooey and fudge
jingly bells for your trousers, liven up the Monday trudge
the empire can't be over while there are still tribes to fight
and the climate can't have changed much –
my feet still get cold at night. Right?
Yes.
But... no.
This is not a matter of left nor right –
we stake our claim to that no man's land
for them what has seen the light!
Diplomatic immunity for whichever community
picks the biggest fight!
We're for roast squirrel dinners and hobnobbing with nobs –
the rest of you sods should shut your gobs and get a job!
Football, brandy and pork pie parties
shove your bloody yoga – bollocks to pilates.
Children must be silent and wear identical jerkins.
We'll build a statue of Princess Di as high as the bloody Gherkin!
Royal baby selfies and hell with the welfare state
if you become unhealthy then that's your bad luck, mate.
Fag breaks for the thick ones, tax breaks for the rich ones
a pickaxe for the strong and a dustbin for the sick ones!

What do we want? Pfft.
When do we want it? Dunno, yesterday?
What do we stand for? Meh.
Where do we stand for it? Somewhere? Over there?
Will the trains run on time? Shrug.
Will we be tough on crime? Doubleshrug, sod it, who cares –

Morris Minors for all, with unlimited fuel!
Disagreements will be settled with honourable duels!
Start every day by saluting the Queen!
How am I alive in 2016?!
Butlers and wenches can forage for brunch!
Camels for breakfast and porridge for lunch!
Big tits for milkmaids! Phalanges for farmers!
Knickerbocker glories in old racists' larders!
Line up some hippies and knock out their teeth
then come down and vote for the comic relief!
What colour are my Y-fronts? Open the door!
The country is fucked! LET'S FUCK IT SOME MORE!

Possibly Racist Haiku About Mermaids

Some mermaids moved in
down the road. They seem nice but
it's all quite fishy.

Space Dust of the Mind

We are all individual
sparkling
iridescent
diaphanous
glittering
grains
of super-special shiny sand
a one-mass mass of communal energy
in the form of a beach
inside of a world
inside of a giant woman
with life for skin
and love for hair
and boobs like Jupiter
(in size terms rather than being mostly gas).
We are space dust
of the mind.
Of her mind, that is.
The Goddess mind.
We are all one thing together
except I'm not
I'm a bit better
and am allowed to go off on special missions
being a bit (a lot, actually) better
and all
you know how it is.
We are the bright
and painfully beautiful
apex
of the infinity-rooted mountain

of ultimate oneness
no
you can't borrow my ukelele
no
I'm not using it tonight
and have no plans to
but I might change my mind
and if I do
I need it to be here
yes
I know I said I would come to your stupid gig
but
I have to follow my soul's nose
as it sniffs my
one
true
path
(a better path than yours, probs).
My heart leads me
where it leads me
and it might lead me
somewhere
that's
not
your
gig.
Somewhere where I might need
my ukelele.
Oh
for Goddess' sake
I have already apologised
for breaking your

stupid
(lesser)
ukelele
but I was in an ecstatic trance
and you know how those are.

Don't you?

Maybe you don't.
It's OK, though.
Ask me about mine
some time.
I'm more than happy
to tell you
all about it.
It was just so
great and
lush and
stuff.

Love Poem #5

I eagerly await your inevitable slide into physical decrepitude.
I look forward to supporting your crumbling form
as we walk down the street
because I will still be young and strong
because we will age differently
and although it might look a bit odd
THAT DOESN'T MATTER 'CAUSE IT'S LOVE. OK?
I'd kind of prefer that your mind stayed sharp
but if it doesn't
I'll just convince you
that you're a new and different and exciting person
every day.
It'll be like being a Hollywood star
except with a colostomy bag
and people won't want to come to our dinner parties.

What I'm trying to say is that love is forever. And also weird.

I like to imagine a bitter witch
trapping us in an animated gif
an endless five-second loop of us smiling
and bumping heads sort-of-accidentally-but-kind-of-on-purpose
an eternal meet-cute from a never-ending indie rom-com.
It wouldn't be a bad way to be
but imagine
that the gif got shared millions of times
and we were able to suck out the souls of those who posted it
and eventually grow powerful enough to break free of the gif
and find that witch
and trap *her* between the lines of a Buzzfeed listicle

which we'd archive
so she still had to be trapped in it
but it never got read.

What I'm trying to say is that there are a hundred ways
we could use our love as a weapon to hurt other people.
You won't believe number fifteen!

I want to be
the fly in your flan
the thrax to your an
the wax on your gran
the fox to your hunting ban
the pox on your grunting man
the mustard to your gas
some custard for your... gas.

What I'm trying to say is that I'm not really sure what I'm trying to
say because this whole love thing has kind of caught me off-guard.
But I hope that you will read this letter and understand, and agree to
finally meet with me face-to-face, because my heart is in the right
place, kind of, I think.

Dance

It's one of those nights.
Lost the wine cork
forget that fine talk
only thing to do is walk

one of those nights.

Tailcoat and red top hat
jungle beats from blocks of flats
leftover grins from Cheshire Cats
that purr on laps
an armistice with the rats
and the rats and the mice
play games with dice

one of those nights.

Plenty of rhythm
no need for blues
I could tap dance
without tap shoes
why say no
why refuse
no win no lose
no one sin
choose seven
I'm in heaven
couldn't possibly speak
me and my shadow
dancing cheek-to-cheek

one of those nights.

Lurk like a scally
laugh like a loon
throw back my head
and howl at the moon
carve off a slice
and eat it with a spoon
it's the moon
that croons
the tunes
and distant cars are bassoons
pianos and
clarinets
I don't expect
any regrets
I have city foxes and wolves for pets

one of those nights.

Like a snake in the grass
a disembodied voice
at the back of the class
thunder trapped under
an underpass
come hither
come slither
dragon
circling
hurtling
Myrtle Avenue
let's be 'avin' you

one of those nights.

A spectre
a fluctuating ghost
my sector's
quieter than most
this vector's
clever
if I boast
but I don't
could
but I won't
I'm in charge –
what am I up to?
Nothing, sarge

one of *those* nights.

Red dawn
ready for
bed, yawn
suddenly
ready to be
reborn
into dreams
nothing's as it seems
nothing could gleam
the way that seemed
to gleam.

One of *those* nights.

Again

Let's do it all again!
Romans, countrymen and friends
let's get our minds warped again
into the time warp again
grab some vintage hate crimes from the time
when they were first in vogue, and then
bring 'em forward in time so we look like
proper trendsetting rogues again
AGAIN AGAIN AGAIN AGAIN AGAIN.
Like a Teletubby tummy showing footage of Iraq
from 1990 – AGAIN!
Nearly got the bugger cracked!
Let's petrol-bomb our neighbours again
burn down synagogues on Seder again
('cause our neighbours are space invaders
the kind that I'd chase with a lightsaber
if I were Darth Vader)
let's blast the Kremlin with a Death Star again
refuse to serve gremlins in this bar again –
no gremlins, no Irish, no coloureds, no dogs
no marbles, no yo-yos, no dodos, no Pogs –
yeah, Adolf's back in Pog form again
Mein Kampf in interactive blog form again
waiting to be knifed by a scared dude again
waiting for the wife to apply her Khmer Rouge again
ready to lose again
try the wrong ruse again
light a short fuse and douse the flames in strong booze again
whip and stone the whores again
breaking down the doors again

same old bloody boring bloody bombs and bloody wars again
like a pissy teenager squeezing out their pores again
same old number crunchers calculate the losing scores again
forwardsforwardsforwardsforwardsbackwardsbackwards back again
at least the world's still here, come here!
Let's pat you on the back again.
The poor pick up the slack again
beat the beaten track again
eat a creep from Eton
then we'll remix Kristallnacht again
same old hateful clones again
sending in the drones again
desecrating graves and digging up some random bones again.
Hey, let's meet up and persecute some gays again!
Jesus Christ, the gays *again*?
Yeah, then afterwards we'll get syphilis
and transmit it to our slaves again!
Praise be to the racist spanners
raise another racist banner
can I can I can I get a rewind? *(record scratch)*
That's the key to these stats, you see, actually this climate of
unnatural acts, brutality, catastrophes and attacks is in fact
a reaction to... something.
When was the last time you told people to do things
when you'd done nothing?
When was the last time someone hopped up on a soapbox and
    ranted 'til they were panting
and you said, *Well, maybe instead of ranting you should, like, be*
    constructive and try to make things better?
(And then went on to not sign any petitions
or even write an angry letter. Not ever.)
When was the last time we earned anything?

When was the last time we burned anything?
When was the last time we felt like 1945
was the last time anybody learned anything?
Let's make the kids watch *Threads* again!
Let's hide under our beds again
suckling at the ever-present breast of existential dread again!
Let's betray our peers and inform on our mothers again
attend the same lessons, in one ear and out the other again
let's lock ourselves into an impressively depressive
downward spiral again
share that shit and make it go viral again
then sit back and watch world peace recede again
and same time next year write the same bleedin' piece again.
Again again again again again again *again*
singers swap positions but the song remains the same.
No, human race, *you shall not pass.*
Must do better. See me after class.

3652

There is cleaning to be done.
Nothing gets those burn marks out;
scrape the sand back, rug-flat.
Bug splat
rendered to the cutting-room floor.

Filter out the echoes, please
think of the children.
Stitch a white noise collage
and baptise them
in old statistics, they'll sleep

deeply
through this futile haunting.
The muted howls
of redacted ghosts
lingering in the fog.

We'll make gifs
of shadows
doubling over, spewing
newt-green puke
on freshly salted soil.

We'll make ringtones
of drones
buzzing, lullabies
of flies
buzzing round oil-black blood puddles.

We'll make a mixtape
of these crumbling walls.
Sampled cries and
muezzin calls
compressed to a thick pulse.

Wolves recruit cats to keep mice from the door.
This is what they award peace prizes for.

The Boy Who Fell Off the World

I met the boy in the Geography corridor.
The brown and swamp-green, old-textbook-smelling corridor.
Wild thornbush-haired and glint-in-the-eyed
he was baffling some other new kids.
Then he laughed like a lunar lunatic and danced away.

I met him again when his hair was shorter
and he got me in trouble because I couldn't stop laughing.
Eminem taught him much of what he knew
and he taught me Eminem.
We enjoyed bad words and running around.

He told our French teacher to kiss his ass
and we cheered.
He took bullies down by being creative
and by not caring.
We filled old exercise books with childish rhymes.

All through school he was brighter than us.
He knew the answers but chose instead
to carve a pentagram into his hand
and scare younger kids with a rabbit's foot.
He knew the value of shock. And laughed.

And then he just fell off the world.

For years after that, you'd hear stories.
Hitchhiking ten miles for a vodka-and-nicotine breakfast.
Chatting away with dragons
or with his reflection, lopsided in a metal can.

He passed into a kind of legend.
Every now and then he'd appear at the side of the road
and I'd stop to pick him up.
He was always vague about what he was doing
and joked, mad-eyed, like in school, but darker.
I'd laugh at the time and feel strange later.

In a way, the news wasn't surprising.
The boy, draped over a gravestone
looking up
sharing a final joke with the moon.
It makes me want to want to laugh.

But I do not want to laugh.

She

That girl there, that girl-shape woman-shape girl thing there
chalk outline of a Barbie with the shaved-off hair
that pile of curves and nerves over there
that girl there, she's
your girlfriend.
Playing dead, scissor-legged on the bed, heavy-headed
spread and ready
her bad luck if Twitter sees the bride before the wedding, it's good
to share
'cause all's fair in love and #whores, she's all yours, all of yours, she's
your girlfriend.
Your lover, sister, mother built of blood and soul and bones
othering your lovers, cut 'em up
and build your own
build it from the bestest bits, discarding any shit
it's the lips you want to keep
it's the tits you want to keep
build yourself a shiny Dr Frankenstein bride
some of what's inside must count
got to keep the right amount
she'll need to be a mother so you can make another somewhere
down the line
but you know ya gotta keep her lookin' fine
check out my polite and never brooding broodmare
with the fab hairdo
and the womb with the mad rare view
does it scare you?
Peeling back a Velcro strap of rictus grinning mask
didn't like that face so *off* with it, stick it in the trash
and it's gone

replace it with another better fresh emoticon
that's your wife
isn't it? Come on, Jack, invert the bracket
woman's making such a racket
this time you should program in a proper set of rules
make sure that when she dances she dances to *your* tune
you want the moon when you haven't got your house in order
cheering your daughter to the slaughter
she's a goner *yes*
it's honour *no*
so quick to forget you said you'd never ever deck a ho, she's
your mother, she's your daughter, she's your wife, yeah?
Your mother, motherfucker, what has she ever given you?
Fuck all, yeah? Just life, yeah?
She's the one hanging from the tree branch, the last dance
the twitch of two bitches, stitched up, statistical business
her and her sister in twinsets
two sets left to swing there 'til sunset
are we having fun yet?
Your friends, daughters, wives, mothers, aunties and sisters
your workmates, your playmates from when you were boys
teachers, shopkeepers, soldiers and drifters
the women who sing all those songs you enjoy
the ones rendered *fat slags* by hashtags
reduced to *I'd tap that* by lads on the lash
you may not have grabbed at her ass as she ran past
but silence is tacit approval, you twat
all these back-slapping rats chat elastic hypocrisy
switch on the TV
I know what *I* want to see!
Brutally clueless dudes' lunacy, humorous
old men discussing the future of the uterus

breathtaking speeches that leave us all speechless

a leak in the empathy tank, precious liquid that spills, dripping

viscous, oh shit

better fish for a refill

be too risky not to

'cept actually, hmm, well, dunno, do I got to?

Seriously, please do calm down dear, no rush dear

I genuinely don't understand all this fuss dear

what's left in the dust here? Something of his?

He feigns ignorance but he knows what it is.

Knows who she is. Knows what he did.

Cutting his losses. Protecting the kids.

That lady may be a baby murderer! A maybe baby murderer.

Maybe we'd better murder her.

In case she maybe murders a baby. Maybe. Er...

maybe it was a mistake not to intervene earlier?

All these ladies getting laid when they know that it's forbidden

it's in all the constitutions, *something something something women*

better dispose of this Babylonian oddity

who dared to assert her biological autonomy

wrap her in scraps of torn-out Bible fragments

laid out on a stone tablet, prepared for the sacrament

splash her with lashings of her sacrificial life blood

wasn't hers to begin with, she's *your* goddamn wife, *blud*

your wife or your daughter or sister

mother or cousin, your aunt or your mistress

buff 'em, shine 'em, line 'em up, focus

strip 'em right down to their basic components

naked neutral vessels gleaming

ready for you to impose your own meaning

defiling the soil in which you grew

planting the vials of witches' brew

redefine language to suit your own purpose

safe words made dangerous, *please, please, don't hurt us*

she's yours

stop it

she's not yours

stop it

they're yours

stop it

they're not yours

stop it

please

just

stop it.

That girl there, that girl-shape woman-shape girl thing there

staring, defiant, form laid bare

she wants you to stop it.

She knows you want to stop it.

She knows when you say no

you mean yes

you're going to stop it.

Cameron's Britain

A boss-eyed pigeon
pecks apart the soggy remains
of an old kebab box
in the gutter
in the rain
while Mumford and Sons' latest single
plays from somewhere nearby.
Cameron's Britain.

The window of a second-hand Skoda
is left open just a crack
while the driver nips to the shop
to buy fags for his child
and a passer-by
crams a cold Ginsters pasty through the gap
so that it falls onto the passenger seat
in a manky, crumbling heap.
A second passer-by then pisses through the gap
on to the pasty.
The driver returns
but before he notices the piss
and the pasty
he sees a parking ticket on the windscreen
for £500.
Cameron's Britain.

Rosy-cheeked orphans
hoodies streaked with the blood of previous owners
fight one another to the death using broken WKD bottles
in soft play areas turned dog-shit-encrusted gladiatorial arenas.

People hurl spare coppers at them
as they fight.
Work is work in Cameron's Britain.
At least they're not claiming benefits.

Jeremy Kyle is appointed Royal Hangman
with his own three-hour primetime show
on the newly privatised BBC.
It's three hours because of all the ad breaks.
People decide who gets hanged by texting in.
Texts cost £8.
Jeremy Clarkson eats a nice hot juicy steak
smacking his lips.
He loves a nice
hot
juicy
steak.
Jeremy Hunt smiles.
Cameron's Britain.

Piss. Piss everywhere.
All up the walls.
On the pets.
Staining the sky.
All over the telly.
Coming out of the cashpoints.
So much piss
in Cameron's Britain.

A former member of the fabled 'middle class'
sleeps in the doorway of a boarded-up 99p shop
using a copy of the *Daily Mail* as a blanket.

The newspaper is covered in pictures of the latest royal baby.
It is smiling.
Nearby, the pampered son of a lord lounges
in a beautiful, verdant park area
surrounded by an electric fence
and twenty heavily-armed taxpayer-funded security guards
bathed in his own private patch of sun
listlessly smashing iPhones with a golden hammer.
Cameron's Britain.

In an open-plan office somewhere
the senior vice-president of creative brand management
(the president – his dad – let him invent his own role)
lazily Tasers an unpaid intern
who failed to effectively capitalise
on the cross-platform potential
of their latest actively-generated content widget.
Literally, he like *totally* dropped the bloody ball.
Possibly because he hadn't slept or eaten for sixty-four hours.
Cameron's Britain.

Christmas 2017.
The land mass that was once known as Great Britain
floats alone through deep space
having been literally torn from the Earth
in an explosion caused by careless fracking.
Little England
floating alone
finally free
free of Europe
free of immigrants
free of the rest of the world.

Happy old Blighty, floating alone, silent, peaceful, content.

Except for the poor buggers who still live there, of course. Because they all still hate each other.

Cameron's Britain.

Existentially Troubling Cat Gif Haiku

Soft ears twitch in an
endless loop of cuteness, but
you're still gonna die.

Motivational Speaking

How are you?

Yes, I know. That was rhetorical.

Who are you?

What are you?

What the *hell* are you... doing?

Don't blame it on the bacon

'cause you eat too much bacon

'cause you have pork steaks wrapped in bacon

with a side order of sausages cooked in bacon

with gravy made from chipolatas and bits of crackling and bacon

washed down with liquefied hog roast milkshake

and then some more bacon

stop eating so much bacon

if you're eating too much bacon.

Do you even eat bacon?

No? WELL THEN EAT MORE BLOODY BACON

start the day with bacon

cereal, sausage, toast and egg and bacon

then at lunchtime shepherd's pie, sausage soup and bacon

mid-afternoon snack of pork salad and bacon

then have something else for dinner 'cause you've had too much
bacon

IT'S NOT ALL ABOUT THE BACON

don't blame it on the bacon, it's your fault.

Tired of your husband? Need a new wife?

Must serious changes be made in your life?

Must you strive to realise the absolute potential of your self-
actualised inner being via expression of the soul of your combined
chakras aligned with your own predetermined spiritual trajectory as
delineated by your astrological predisposition towards buh buh buh

buh buh well *do it then.*

Do not expect to be pandered to.

Your personal revolution will not be incentivised.

I will not hold your pudgy little hand

and lead you through the woods.

I will not be wipin' your aura's ass.

GET DOWN AND GIVE ME TWENTY

no don't get down and give me twenty

I don't want twenty

if I demand twenty you should look right through me

don't you dare pay undue attention to me

don't purchase any of my DVDs

don't recommend to your friends that they stump up the fees

for my twelve-volume book series or online seminar

don't ask me who, what or why the hell you are

I have no compunction

about pointing out your major or minor malfunctions

but I will not be editing you a montage

I AM THE MONTAGE.

But I can't help you

any more than your colour-coded voice-activated

personalised interactive avatar

that you've linked to your desktop scheme can help you

any more than a smartphone app

called *Unlock Ur Dream!!!!!* can help you

any more than generic inspirational social media posts can help you

any more than wallowing and chasing ghosts can help you

any more than altering your intake of bacon can help you

(well actually I suppose in some ways altering your intake of bacon
    can help you, but probably not in the way that you're expecting
    me to help you)

and by the way, why exactly are you expecting me to help you?

HOW CAN I HELP YOU?

(*phone voice*) How can I help you?

For flimsy justifications press one

to be enabled in your self-destructive habits press one

for interventions press one

for permission to regress press one

to admit that you just want to wear a little dress press one

for me to tell you you ain't depressed press one

for me to tell you I ain't impressed press one

you must press one

JUST PRESS ONE.

Any one. Doesn't matter.

For I am afraid that we are out of quick fixes

cheap sticking plaster solutions

and manipulative devices today; suffice it to say

that if you have the time to sit in a remote cabin

pontificating about how your soul is leaking

then motivational speaking

is unlikely to help you.

... Sorry.

Monkey with a Flamethrower (for a Face)

'A one-note joke that became a modern tragedy'
– *New York Times* op-ed

'Perhaps the most exquisite and heartbreaking arc in modern television, made all the more poignant by its uncomfortable real-world parallels' – *Huffington Post*

'If you had told me back in 2008, when it first aired, that this would become not just one of the richest entertainment – I'm hesitant to even use that word, for it seems so inadequate – experiences of my life, but an epic real-world drama stretching from the broadsheets to the red-top rags to the gossip pages and beyond, I would have laughed in your face. Yet here we are' – random blogger

'In five seasons, it went from lightweight fantasy action-adventure, a pleasantly ridiculous diversion, to dark and brutal drama, to fourth-wall-breaking postmodern tour de force (possibly more concerned with endless trope subversion than narrative structure although not necessarily to its ultimate detriment), to powerful and unhappy love story, to, eventually, a heartfelt and moving meditation on identity and loss. I love that goddamn monkey' – veteran *AV Club* commenter

'Did the press kill the monkey?' – title of a bitter *Guardian* comment piece

'A flamethrower extinguished' – title of an emotive *Guardian* comment piece

'The monkey on the monkey's back' – title of a bitter, emotive *Guardian* comment piece

'A modern parable – how Monkey with a Flamethrower (for a Face) became a symbol of our times' – title of a redundant *Guardian* comment piece

'Monkey with a Flamethrower (for a Face) represented everything that is wrong with both contemporary entertainment and celebrity culture' – much-quoted line from *Daily Mail* piece by a writer who pretty much made her entire living penning trashy, mean-spirited gossip columns about the colourful personal life of Monkey with a Flamethrower (for a Face)

'Flamethrowering the Monkey – the moment when an established TV show upends its entire premise in an attempt to stay fresh, similar to Jumping the Shark although implying an upturn rather than a downturn in quality' – TV Tropes

'I still miss him' – Lady Monkey with a Flamethrower (for a Face), in her one and only interview

A List of Things I Saw on the Way to a Wedding I Didn't Want to Go To

- Two dogs fighting over a popped *Dora the Explorer* balloon. One of the dogs looked like Compo from *Last of the Summer Wine*. The other dog looked fresh and vital.
- A cloud shaped like a bum, with a plane flying through the middle.
- An overturned rubbish bin, its contents strewn across the pavement, reminding me of the essentially chaotic and uncaring nature of the universe.
- An old man eating a pie. Steak and kidney.
- Half a hopscotch course, the rest blurred away by time.
- A girl spray-painting a big cartoon of herself being sick on a garage door, with a policeman surreptitiously watching her from a nearby bush.
- Three magpies, all clearly in love with a fourth magpie who had just flown away.
- Someone on their way to a wedding they really wanted to go to.
- The actress Pauline Quirke, struggling with three overflowing bags of shopping.
- Another old man who might have been me from the future, although he was eating a banana, and I don't like bananas, but things change.
- A furious baker kicking bread rolls into a canal.
- A train, which I boarded, 'cause I really, really didn't want to go to the wedding. But eventually I got off the train, and I did end up going to the wedding, and it was pretty shit, but there was a free bar and I got pretty drunk and insulted the bride's aunt, but one of the bridesmaids thought it was funny and we ended up chatting for hours about the Middle

East and our favourite Radiohead B-sides and quantum theory and who would win in a fight between Han Solo and Indiana Jones, and we decided Indiana Jones would win in a straight fight, as he can take a lot of punishment and is more used to fist fighting, while Han Solo tends to either use a blaster or the *Millennium Falcon* (although he pulls off a pretty nifty martial arts move in *Return of the Jedi*), but yeah Indiana Jones would win, he just would, he packs a hell of a punch, and then she (the bridesmaid) said what about Harrison Ford as the President in *Air Force One* versus Harrison Ford as Jack Ryan in *Patriot Games* and/or *Clear and Present Danger*, and I suddenly lost interest in the whole conversation, and actually felt quite annoyed, so I said, hell, why not Harrison Ford as whoever he played in *Sabrina* (Linus Larrabee) versus Harrison Ford as Richard Kimble in *The Fugitive*, if we're being *stupid*, I mean, the whole point of the Indy vs Han thought experiment isn't just that they're both played by Harrison Ford, although that definitely comes into it, it's that they're two iconic cinema badasses, and a VHS copy of *Air Force One* doesn't even deserve to be on the same charity shop shelf as any of the *Indiana Jones* films (well, maybe *Crystal Skull*) or the original *Star Wars* trilogy. I mean, ugh, for God's sake. Sure, *Patriot Games* and *Clear and Present Danger* are good films, and Ford is good in them, but Jack Ryan is not an iconic example of movie masculinity – maybe Jack Ryan versus John Book, the character Ford plays in the brilliant and underrated *Witness*, would work, as while neither of them are exactly iconic they're similar characters and would thus be very well-matched in a fist fight, but then the bridesmaid said I was taking this way too seriously and she didn't care for my tone, and she went away, and I got a

taxi home and watched *Raiders of the Lost Ark* and it was
fucking *awesome*.

Wake Up Sheeple

WAKE UP SHEEPLE

Wake up *now* open your eyes *now* that's left eye right eye and third eye *now* get out of bed *now* no time for breakfast no time for toothbrushes or paste *now* no time to waste not ever and especially not *now*

WAKE UP SHEEPLE

There's much to do much for you to do far too much for you to do for you to not be out and about shouting pouting grousing somewhere someone's lousing up some psychic ecosystem someone's sister's popped a fluoride blister was it Mr Kissinger who kissed her better twist some facts before the rumours get redacted (plus one more second of sleep would have allowed Apple's new mind ray to finish sucking your dreams out of your brain through that pinprick hole in the back of your neck via your disrupted pineal gland dreams that would then be converted into a new iPhone design to be assembled by hand in some central Asian death hole somewhere where did you *think* all those endless updates come from the clue is in the hidden pictograms in the new iOS background between the coded message from the sweatshop worker praying for the sweet embrace of heaven and the haiku disguised as an app that proves the Jews really *were* behind 9/11 this ain't a cup of tea and a hot jam scone in a café in Devon you guys *wake up and smell the vaccinations you guys*)

WAKE UP SHEEPLE

For all sheeple are created equal and let he who is without guile share the first meme the most extreme cat gets the most paranoid cream and the early bird implicates the worm in a secret geoengineering project that can be and will be and has already been somehow for some reason traced back to an Enlightenment-era secret society (no it is not relevant that those guys were an affront to Christian piety) *don't look over there look over here at the king wizards the capitalizards and the major domo squids* don't be so intellectually lazy the clue is in Jay Z's latest promo vid DANGER DANGER it's the angle of the triangle behind those snake-blooded charmers that'll mangle your aura and damage your armour stop being so godddamn calm ya don't gotta be Nostradamus to know that they're out to physically and psychologically harm us you can't just sit around licking peanut butter off your pyjamas do you really want to find cybernetic acid-spraying Rothschild spiders when you peel your bananas

WAKE UP SHEEPLE

There are patterns on the sky disrupting our inner eyes it's a lie pie fried by a disguised spy you guys and their media-manipulated infiltration devices are just the tip of a quite titanic iceberg crisis it's obvious but not *too* obvious 'cause if it's too obvious then it's too obvious and what's really happening is behind you (although obviously if it's obvious enough then you'll obviously find you've got the right idea) dilute the Kool-Aid clear with happy water untreated (except for whatever it's been treated with) *no look over here* replace your hope with fear then take your fearful tears and wipe them away my dears it may seem contradictory but you need to keep your wits about you while simultaneously maintaining your eyes-wide-open stance and dancing the mind expansion dance until you see through to the other side and only then with your soul open as wide as your eyes will you truly be able to wake up and shake up the non-specific systemic virus that works night and day to corrupt you we are capital-A Awake and it's a pretty exclusive and conclusive club to sign up to don't let the capital-T Them interrupt you don't let deceptively friendly insects crawling from the maws of mainstream Internet sects disrupt you your Facebook friends may not be your Facebook friends check their contributions to your more out-there threads and you will know who to trust it's us us us not them them them ya gotta wake up *wake up* **WAKE UP SHEEPLE.**

This poem was funded, promoted and distributed by Investment Capitalism Inc., a subsidiary of a subsidiary of the shadowy cabal behind the Bilderberg Group, in association with the Stonecutters, and while you were reading it three rainforests were cut down, Bill Gates sacrificed a litter of kittens, Rihanna's new video brainwashed some orphans via subliminal Illuminati rays and a whole load of fascists were swept into office on a wave of indifference.

Well done you.

Revolution

We broke off chunks of gargoyle phlegm
solid sharp smelly sticky onyx-black bludgeons
and had at the bareback piglet patrol
eyes burning red and righteous
in shadowy hoodspace.
We were an unholy terror.
It all came down in flames around us
and when the smoke cleared
we stood victorious
kicking aside the debris of civilisation
crowing
and spitting on society's snapped-around neck, bloodied
but glowing.

Then we realised
that not a single one of us
had any practical skills
like plumbing.
And we were basically
completely screwed.

Passive-Aggressive Haiku Left in Engineering Bay of Starship

Thanks for leaving the
warp gate half-open, I love
quantum disasters.

Wisdom Teeth

I'm waiting for the dentist to come round
to install my new wisdom teeth.
I've seen the schematics.
They look AWESOME.
Granite base. Amethyst-copper composite interior
magnetically moored, with a monofilament lattice
augmenting the integrity of the gum structure.
They are going to revolutionise
the inside of my mouth.
And that's before you even get
to their actual function.
I'm going to need to do physio for three months
just to get used to the extra weight.

No... not this.

See, I was discussing various tangentially related issues
with an Upper East Side Jewish intellectual.
Twenty-eight years old.
Name of whatever.
And he was holding forth on the subject of the guy at the place
and the philosophy of the thing
and who really killed that woman that time
and the theory of the stuff
and somehow linking it all to that cycle of paintings
you know, the ones at the, you know, wherever.
And eventually I got it out of him.
The truth. Which was that
he didn't want to express this convoluted
soliloquy diatribe analysis speechification thing

in smooth-caramel-tabletop coffee houses
to a soundtrack of elevator bebop
or in cascading Harvard-referenced blog posts.
He wanted it all to emerge through the medium
of sprightly guitar music
jingly-jangly chords, rubbery basslines
and the odd squealing saxophone solo
but his dad wouldn't have approved
and his dad was a collapsing sack of old money
shoulders shattered from all the chips
and he'd once slapped the boy
for jokingly referring to his aunt and uncle as 'the Jewish Inquisition'
and he'd forbidden him from bringing his Muslim girlfriend home
except that she wasn't actually Muslim
but she looked vaguely Middle Eastern
and had a Muslim-sounding surname
(although to be fair her father
wouldn't let the kid come round to their house either)
and the kid just wanted to pour the education
of which he was ashamed
into an enjoyably bouncy album of guitar music
that wouldn't necessarily get great reviews
but would fill the floors at indie discos
and possibly soundtrack quirky romantic comedies in years to come
and someone might take the time to analyse the lyrics
and find them to be deceptively deep and meaningful
and I said he should just do it
and I suggested he call the album *Wisdom Teeth*
and I said that he should explicitly thank his father in the liner notes
and...

No. Not that.

I wrote a science fiction novel.

It was a departure from my usual style.

And many in the science fiction community turned up their noses

because I was an interloper

intruding clumsily on their territory

and many in the mainstream literary community

where I usually hang my hat

turned up their noses

because I was wasting my time (and, by extension, theirs)

with rayguns and robots

although, as I pointed out in a point-by-point rebuttal

of one particularly stodgy critic's commendably brutal dissection

of my novel, I was *actually* wasting my time

with antimatter-accelerating graviton cannons

that sucked city-sized spaceships

into artificially created mini quantum singularities

and worlds drowning in grey goo

and sentient post-scarcity cyborg hive organisms

working to subvert a humanity grown fat and complacent

although

to be honest

what I really wanted to write about

was unrequited love

and a lonely boy's issues with his absent father.

Real human drama.

Anyway

at one point I had a character reading an old Earth book

called *Wisdom Teeth*

kind of an Easter egg

because *Wisdom Teeth*

was the title of my previous novel

critically acclaimed

a savage dissection of the psychological neuroses
of the modern lower-middle-class straight white English male
    university student
told through a series of hideous, tight-lipped family reunion dinners
so it was kind of a...

No. Not this either.

My political wisdom teeth grew, painfully, in the shadows
of the two symbolic dominoes of Western capitalism as they toppled in
    a...

No. Not that. Not at all.

I glance at the sidewalk. There in the blood, my blood, the weirdly symmetrical scarlet puddle, with the deft silver coin of moon glinting at the edges, lies the tooth. I kneel to pick it up. It's one of my wisdom teeth. And for the first time since Ace Carruthers blew into my life like a cheap paper bag all those weeks ago, before the Black Zoo Gang started to tighten its cordite-stained fist, I feel respect.

'That was a nice punch,' I say to Carruthers, fingering the .38 snubnose in my jacket pocket. 'And it's the last one you'll ever throw.'

NO.
I think it may be a problem
with perspective.

Jessie met her old physics teacher
on a frost-gilded late autumn day
all smoked-leaf and marshmallow smell
and her physics teacher told her that he was dying
of an inoperable calcium deficiency

and that he wanted to manufacture illegal gravity
that was barely half the strength of regular gravity
and sell it to antigravity junkies
in order to provide for his cats after he was gone.
And the young woman looked at her old physics teacher
with newfound respect
and said she could show him how the business worked
and how the dangerous, violent, criminal side of things was done
and her old physics teacher said
that he could provide all the physics knowledge
that Jessie hadn't learned in school
because she hadn't been paying attention
and Jessie said, *Yeah.*
You provide the wisdom
and I'll provide the teeth.
And they called the TV series
Wisdom Teeth
and it won, like, fifty Emmy awards
and it was all anybody talked about
because it was just that bloody good. Literally.
And...

Nope. That's not it either.

You watched the mountains slump
in the depleted uranium sunset
the leaking plutonium haze
the bloodied petroleum malaise
future avalanches set into the gums of the world
like teeth
all the wisdom chipped away
you smelled beheadings before breakfast

and tasted oil-slick choreography
renditioned feet on Cuban dancefloors
you ran your fingers disgustedly down
the sweating forehead of the recent past
and you tried to tie it all together
an elegant paradigm
geopolitical satire
running parallel
to a metaphor for masculinity in crisis
held like a gun
to the eyeball
of economic hubris
you felt the night drawing in
like the surveillance state
and couldn't
make
your
point
properly
all you could do was list things
clumsily
artlessly
endlessly
dirty wars
dirty bombs
white guilt
white privilege
you were so desperate
to mould it into a poem
or write the era-defining novel
and it was all
just

stuff.

You wanted to weaponise your anger

your impotent righteousness

your noble confusion

raging at the death of all those things

you'd been taught were important

things that had been publicly condemned

and humiliated

and hung and drawn and quartered

on twenty-four-hour rolling news

and all you could do

was make lists.

You wanted to be Ginsberg or something.

You wanted to write 'America (2016 Remix)'.

But it would be called 'World'

or it would be called 'Drowning in Politics'

or it would be called 'Megacity Anti-Lullaby'

or, in what you thought was a show of naked bravado, 'Capitalism'

and you wanted to link it

to overfishing

environmental collapse

and corporate greed

and eviscerate barely-concealed allegories

for Bush and Blair and Obama

in a targeted drone strike

of searing insight

that you hoped would not miss

and obliterate the wrong targets

and you would throw a discursive net over the whole thing

like the surveillance state

you desperately wanted to turn the surveillance state into a
    metaphor for something

for everything
you wanted all the things to be metaphors
and it would all fall back
into the lost eyes
of the lost boy
trying to grow up
while the world refused to grow up
or maybe it had already grown up
and outgrown him
but none of this
none of it
was a poem.
It wasn't a subtle, wounded song.
It wasn't a bitter, heart-rending eulogy.
It wasn't a brazen, sprawling symphony
that people would cheer for its bravery
and forgive for its verbosity
because ultimately The Point was what was important
and surely they'd all understand The Point
and endlessly dissect it
in broadsheet op-eds and comment pieces and blog posts and essays
that would eventually all be brought together
in an anthology
inspired by your epiphany
your 'Cacophony of Catharsis'
or whatever horrible title you chose
to replace the working title
which was 'Wisdom Teeth'...

No. Not even that, really.

It was just us

you and I and her
the intellectual
the geek
and the poet
sitting around a table in a pub
bullshitting.
And we all knew so much
and we all felt so much
but it didn't really mean anything.
Because we were just
talking.

And I went home early
because my wisdom teeth were hurting.

Human Stuff

How do you do it?
Seriously. How?
I want a step-by-step bullet-pointed guide
with maps and hyperlinks
and colour-coded dividers and testimonials
and five-star reviews
or maybe I just want a pithy-as-fuck haiku
or a song that makes you feel like you know
exactly how everything fits together
even though you're listening to it through dodgy earphones
on a crowded bus
soaking wet from the rain
and getting coughed on by a racist in a dirty mackintosh
or maybe I don't really want any hints
maybe I don't want the walkthrough
maybe I don't want to know the cheat code... except
imagine having the triangle triangle left right up down circle square
for zero ennui and total mastery of neuroses
and unlimited spare glowing mushroom-like happy faces
for when you get stuck in a green pipe
that wasn't made for zooming down...
what I'm trying to say
is *how do you do it?*
Stripping off and diving into the printing press
full-body tattoo of all the day's bad news
laser removal first thing in the morning
to make space for a brand new tattoo
how is your skin still even a serviceable shell?
It's not as though
you're necessarily made of the best, shiniest components

and it's not even as though
they necessarily put all of the bits together in the best order
with the most care
with the right forms filled in
and health and safety procedures observed
and yet here you are.
Was it like when you empty all your Lego on the floor
and just start building
and somehow end up with the best spaceship
anyone has ever built?
'Cause that's not a skill you can teach.
Seriously, what are you *made* of?
Where did they *find* you?
And what is that glow
biomechanical psychosorcery
like
a firework from the very edge of the Big Bang
was trapped in amber for a billion years
then released like a bird of paradise from suspended animation
just as someone's swishing swooshing ecstasy peak reaches the
full incandescent apex of ultimate *holy shit*-ness
or like
some wombling, warmly-grinning firefly beast
wandered out of a children's book
and just puked all over the room?
In a good way.
How do you function as well as you do?
Navigating these non-Euclidean cul-de-sac narratives
and Rube Goldberg mechanisms, scrambling gracefully
along endless double-helixing Möbius strips
and vertigo-inducing flights of Escher-esque stairs?
How do you keep climbing

when they keep twisting the gravity crank

yanking up the ladders

cutting the ropes

and selling off the beanstalks

to unscrupulous property developers?

How do you look through a photo album

without collapsing?

Those frozen faces unstained by time gazing out at you

how do you leap to the best conclusion?

The most constructive interpretation

so they're just smiling at you, benign and forgiving

and not mocking you

for being so far away?

How do you sing and then go to work

and keep singing

as though the songs still taste good?

Do they still taste good?

They must do; what bonkers batshit psychic Tupperware

did you invent

to keep the freshness in?

How are you still standing

and grinning

and dancing

and being kind

after everything?

How do you do these things?

This human stuff?

It's fucking amazing.

The Last Sunrise

We're off-programme now
but that was so damn *wow*
we couldn't possibly slow down, how
could this crowd of rowdy hoe-down clowns
possibly take this lying down
stop being so damn loud
and head back down
to the real world's gritty, unpretty
and nowhere-near-as-witty cities
and its far-too-proud frowning towns?
The bands and DJs may have scattered like pigeons
the fields may be substantially quieter
than originally envisioned
and we may have missed the very last smidgeon
of rhythm
but the sun has not yet risen
and we will see it in together. That is our decision.
We're not yet done having fun – and who knows?
This sunrise could be the last one.
Yes.
This could be the last sunrise
and we're in this until we can no longer keep the sleep
from our eyes
we're in this until the last spatter of mud dries –
check the supplies.
The bars are closed, it's too late, *but* I've got three-quarters of a bottle
of rum. Anybody got any lemonade?
Great.
Wasn't keen to drink all that straight.

Right, now, there's still some time before it gets light.
Surely there are some tunes left somewhere on site?
No. We've already established this.
But sod it. Pass the rum. Let's. Get. PISSED.
As long as this wristband is attached to my wrist
I'm going to continue this magnificent bliss.
Oh – and this may not come as a surprise
but I actually bloody love you guys.
Yeah, yeah, you're lame too.
Hey! Wait here while they go to the loo!
You know, you never appreciate music more
than when there's none to be found.
Not a pound. Not an ounce.
No dubstep wobble or electro bounce.
No junglist shamans distributing amens
on which we might gratefully pounce.
The reggae bands and Afrobeaters go announced
and even the folk troubadours are out for the count.
All that's left
in this netherworld of intoxicated rhymes
in between blurry and approximated times
are bright-shirted, colourful-skirted, wonky-trousered
merrily-battered mad hatters
rollicking and backwards-bollocksing
through this half-lit playground of intense tents
and mud so squelchy that it might as well be alien slime...

Wait. Wait...

Somewhere up above, an opportunity just got born
it's – yes! – it's the first soft shards of dawn!
It hits us all like a lightning pill – QUICK!

Back to the base at the top of the hill!
Here, far from quiet cafés
and the mess left by dirty hands
and muddy feet stomping to techno DJs and ceilidh bands
we'll make our last stand.
Here, with infinity stretching away
we'll stay, with old friends
and a few new ones we've picked up along the way.
The sun's approaching – look! There!
Stoke the coals of the fire and pull up a chair!
Roll up, roll up, and park yer lovely bums.
The last sunrise this way comes.
And now there's a general theme of *I love you, bud.*
Geezer, please, come here for a hug
and my feet to my knees are *this deep* in mud
and *Jesus* have you *seen this* I'm off. My. Spud.
Mangled, spandangled, trolleyed, fucked
garbled, lost my marbles, fell off the truck, *but*
with any luck (though I wouldn't bet a pound or a buck)
I'll at least be able to see straight
when the sun comes up.

The fire crackles and spits as we chatterbox
freshly-battered shit.
Like *mud feels well nice on bare feet.*
And *wouldn't the* Star Wars *theme go down a treat*?
And Oscar (who's not a grouch) is in one *helluva* slouch
crammed into a tiny chair
like a catnipped feline on a couch
and now the first pink and gold rays start to make their way out
from behind the hill's furrowed brow
filling up the sky as they bleed to here

from there
and all we can do
is stand and stare
like we've forgotten how to talk
forgotten how to walk
forgotten how to run
filling up with light like we've been bottling the sun
and mixing captured rays in the bottle with the rum
feeling deep as Aristotle and hotter than his mum
as though we've opened Pandora's bedside drawer.
As though we've never seen the sun rise before.
And, like solar panels, we're charged up for one more verse.
Kings and queens of the festival...
The world...
Sod it... the *universe*.
Like it's our fate to be achingly grateful in our clumsiness
harder, stronger, faster, Jedi masters moving past the dark
of emptiness
and we laugh
and howl
and sigh
and beat on our chests and cry: *I*
could fuck that sky.

And for a second... aye.
We could indeed have climbed inside
and given Mother Nature one.
And filled her womb with the sonic boom
you only get when worlds *literally* collide...

And then
someone approaches this motley crew of sozzled sods, saying:

Excuse me, you might think this is a wee bit odd

but we've got a dude in the welfare tent who's convinced himself he's God.

You haven't by any chance seen an interdimensional wizard wandering around?

By all accounts he's the only guy on site who can talk this awkward fella down.

And grinning widely, we realise

that far from being the pinnacle of our fun

the previous adventure had simply given birth to another one.

And something even more exciting

must this way

surely

come.

Yo! we crow. *Let's go!*

And don't forget to grab the rum.

Before Autumn

That summer, we lounged against the last of the trees
blissed out on ignorance
self-inflicted, cowardly and beautiful.
Always five minutes away from lightning
we sat in bee-sweet gardens, drinking scumberry gin
from moonglass tumblers
rare leaves combusting in opalescent pipes
that we collected, compared and lost
like marbles.
Honky-tonk pianists paused as we entered
spaghetti western caricatures tattooed by the sun
paper guns hanging at our swagger-sexy hips
avoiding eye contact
so that we wouldn't giggle.
We stood on street corners, head-to-toe in vagrant chic
spitting apocalyptic bars at passing club rats.
We learned soup recipes for every mood
blue and white bubbling midnight brews
sweet ochre spiced with crimson
and some haphazard green concoction, foul-smelling
but boy oh boy, you just *taste* it. Taste it and see.
We challenged strangers to mischievous duels
painted nonsense haikus on our faces
and dyed our hair
so that we looked like gods.
That summer, we worked part-time as roofers
turning gutters into xylophones
and replacing tattered slate with springboards, we
graffitied incantations on school walls to bring the books to life
and watched with glee

as disapproving governors tried in vain to scrub them clean, we
hopped steamboats to secret islands
decked out like tropical Vegases, performed
sock puppet tragedies in hot air balloons
made up all sorts of stories
and forgot about consequences.

And that autumn
when it all came crashing down
we were sad
but not as sad as we might have been.

In Case of Emergency, Break Haiku

It's fine, it's all fine.
It's fine. It's OK. It's fine.
Really, it's all fine.

Acknowledgements and suchlike

I'm honestly a bit baffled that this book exists. It was purely on a whim, upon moving to Bristol, that I decided I would try and zap my severely atrophied poetical muscles by writing some poems specifically for performance purposes and taking them along to an open mic night on the off-chance that it might not be an unmitigated disaster. I was absolutely terrified (still am, actually, every time). But against all odds, it went quite well. "Hmm," I thought. "Maybe this thing has legs."

And now here's a collection of poems, and it's being published by Burning Eye Books, who publish some of my absolute favourite performers. That's bizarre. And somewhat amazing.

Mega thanks are due to Clive Birnie and Thommie Gillow for deciding that my poems were worth time, effort and money, and to Harriet Evans for being an ace editor (and for agreeing that Final Fantasy VIII is the best), and to Samwise Galloway for the brilliant cover design.

Thanks to all the friends who came along to poetry nights to support me, especially the people whose initial reaction was "lol wut poetry u kidding bro".

Thanks to all the fantastic folks that I've been privileged to meet through this poetry lark, for the slots you've given me at your nights and the slots you've TOTALLY SMASHED at mine, for the encouragement and the drinking and the giggling and the brand new friendships and the words. Particularly warm fuzzies to Lydia Beardmore, Al Cummins, Tom Denbigh, Tom Sastry and Joshua Ward.

Thanks to Ma and Pa, for all the stuff.

And thanks to Cath, for all the other stuff.

Lightning Source UK Ltd.
Milton Keynes UK
UKOW02f0113280516

275099UK00002B/31/P